The Boxer of Quirinal

Also by John Barr

The War Zone

Natural Wonders

The Dial Painters

Centennial Suite

The Hundred Fathom Curve

Grace

The Hundred Fathom Curve: New & Selected Poems

The Adventures of Ibn Opcit

Dante in China

The Boxer of Quirinal

poems

John Barr

🐓 Red Hen Press | *Pasadena, CA*

Photograph on page 65 "Masses of Christmas Island Red Crabs spawning on the beach." used by permission of Nature Picture Library / Alamy Stock Photo.

Library of Congress Cataloging-in-Publication Data

Names: Barr, John, 1943– author.
Title: The boxer of quirinal: poems / John Barr.
Description: First Edition. | Pasadena, CA: Red Hen Press, [2023]
Identifiers: LCCN 2022038036 (print) | LCCN 2022038037 (ebook) | ISBN 9781636280912 (hardcover) | ISBN 9781636281049 (paperback) | ISBN 9781636280929 (ebook)
Subjects: LCGFT: Poetry.
Classification: LCC PS3552.A731837 B69 2023 (print) | LCC PS3552.A731837 (ebook) | DDC 811/.54—dc23/eng/20220829
LC record available at https://lccn.loc.gov/2022038036
LC ebook record available at https://lccn.loc.gov/2022038037

The National Endowment for the Arts, the Los Angeles County Arts Commission, the Ahmanson Foundation, the Dwight Stuart Youth Fund, the Max Factor Family Foundation, the Pasadena Tournament of Roses Foundation, the Pasadena Arts & Culture Commission and the City of Pasadena Cultural Affairs Division, the City of Los Angeles Department of Cultural Affairs, the Audrey & Sydney Irmas Charitable Foundation, the Meta & George Rosenberg Foundation, the Albert and Elaine Borchard Foundation, the Adams Family Foundation, Amazon Literary Partnership, the Sam Francis Foundation, and the Mara W. Breech Foundation partially support Red Hen Press.

First Edition
Published by Red Hen Press
www.redhen.org

Gratitude

My thanks to the editors who first published the following:

Allium: "Albatross"; *Innisfree Poetry Journal*: "Dante at Shiloh," "The Power & Light Company," "Water's Way"; *Measure: A Review of Formal Poetry*: "Promethean"; *Medmic*: "Hospice, Morristown NJ"; *Poetry*: "The Hove"; *Querencia Anthology*: "L'Envois"; *Scottish Poetry Library*: "The Library of Innerpeffray"; *The Century Association* for setting "Albatross" to music and performing it; *The National Geographic Society*: "Chicago, Tell Me Who You Are"; *The New Criterion*: "Season of Spores"; *The New York Times*: "Heron"; *The Shore*: "Hospice, Morristown NJ"; and *War, Literature & the Arts*: "Black Powder."

With special thanks to Nate, Lisbeth, and William Kinsolving for their readings of "The South China Sea"; to Colby Devitt and Sarah Katz for giving the poems an online life; and to Ilya Kaminsky and Jim Haines, who improved the whole book.

for Ilya Kaminsky

Contents

I. Proof of Life

II. The Boxer of Quirinal

III . The Immortality Sweepstakes

The Boxer of Quirinal

I

Proof of Life

Heron

for Warren Douglas

He comes when the light is right,
banking the pond's perimeter
to land and step into a statue's stillness.

When the light is right the fish come in to feed,
feeling it safe to nose among the weeds,
to risk the proximity of feet, of legs
that rise like reeds to a distant body above.

Once I saw him come in heavy rain,
knowing it would roil the fisheye view.
I watched his neck—a question mark—release,
his beak harpoon a startled shape,
and saw it go headfirst down the hatch.

Perfect hunger. Perfect hunter. Perfect prey.
I wait for the heron to come.

Albatross

For its first five years the bird does not return to land.

Home is not land's end,
a fledgling nest
of food and rest.

Home is the wind
you glide, the sea
you glean unendingly

until a hunger comes
to *Wheel* and *Go*—
not *Home*

but what you can't yet know:
the clambering of kind
on kind.

Eight Minutes Out

Like a ringmaster in the center ring
he keeps the planets circling perfectly;
the comets he allows to have their fling
but brings them back precisely on the day;
the asteroids trumpet and kneel on cue
while all the while he sends his radiance
to neighbor stars, across the Milky Way,
and on into the boundless provenance.

Hardly important—even worth noticing,
if a sliver of his bounty, minutes out,
barely 90 million miles away,
should in its last ten feet change anything—
even if extracting life from light,
a green exception to a winter's day.

L'Envois

Spiders aren't the only things to swing
from silk. Their moment come, the green
half-inch of inchworms dangles everywhere.

They lower of themselves like diving
bells, each fitted out and self-contained
for travels in the perpendicular.

But the green prodigious lowering
must also be in common comprehension
of a destiny they share.

Whatever home is to a driven thing,
they're not there yet but in the in-between,
the neither here nor there.

Some will ascend their silkenism, gaining
again the leaf whereon they eat and spin
and rise like angels to the nth power.

And some will not, falling
prey to the pattern and design
of Heaven-sent grub, forest fare.

God of the Shine, the Brought-Up Boy,
Author of Reverses and Comeuppance,
will your agents rise like booms from below
or will the danglers make it home?
Zero-sum but not a game,
you answer Yes. Yes. Yes.

Season of Spores

One rain and they appear.
Along the trails—*Tranquil Bluff,*
Croghan, Juniper—
a cadence of feeding on the forest floor.

The scatter of moon-colored stuff
erupts from the mire, unfurls
a bric-a-brac of fluke and ruff,
lavender cap, topiary puff.

But no morels!
This field of mortal fruit
battens on decomposing soils,
is only good for witches' spells—

and fun. Architects of the minúte,
a fleet of tiny galleons sails;
a solitary minaret
warns the faithless of their fate.

All rubbery flesh and radial gills,
so alien to what we know,
they are strange to the kingdom of chlorophyll
as marsupial to mammal.

We call out their colors—*gamboge, ecru*—
give them lofty airs—
Whose woods these are they think they know.
But what they do, and do with a will, is grow.

Outriders
    from a parallel universe.
        Foragers. Reconnoiterers.

Book of Knowledge

There's Orion . . . Sirius . . . Mars . . .

Why do you always have to name things?
The fresh experience is enough for me.

Ptolemy was here.
Star simple, fixed on its sphere
in a nest of spheres, each one
moving, Aristotle said,
by the love of its god.

Planes on final, satellite
in transit,
Red Shift, black holes,
dark matter's mass,
the next eclipse.

Is knowledge proximity?
Distance possibility?
Is ignorance bliss?

The Governing Reality

Every man is born an Aristotelian or a Platonist.
—Coleridge

Is it the hammer in Aristotle's hand—
the actual ball-peen, sledge, or maul—

or the ghostly one in Plato's Cave?
His Republic had no place

for poetry's mimetic madness—
but poets had no place for him.

I must lie down where all the ladders start
In the foul rag and bone shop of the heart.

The Möbius Strip

That day she put our heads together,
Fate had her imagination about her,
Your head so much concerned with outer,
Mine with inner, weather.

—Robert Frost

What if there's not a strict divide
Between the two realities?
Möbius took a paper strip,
Twisted it once then glued the ends.
The figure a poem makes likewise mends,
Along the loop of its seamless trip,
Inner and *outer*: as our two eyes
Make one in sight, they coincide.

The Hoard

A weekend seeker, sweeping his detector
through abandoned fields, hears the tone.
Digging deep he finds no urn of coins,
penannular pins, but a box—locked

and full of unsigned poems. Words
beaten thin and fitted to a face;
the shaped whistle of a master's voice
from a world not ours—overheard.

Fascicles in an Amherst attic,
bulls on cave walls in Dordogne:
Troves of inner gold, hidden—
but why? And if not us, who for?

The Library at Innerpeffray

The first lending library in Scotland.

On a drumlin by the River Earn
we step into the nature of the known.
Harled and slated as it was from the start,
this place, its books and the bookmaker's art
for 300 years and counting kept their troth
with crises of loyalties, religious wrath,
rational enquirers and divines,
successive reaches of related minds
to give a shape to reality itself.
Knowledge ages. Shelf by silent shelf
the volumes speak volumes about dead languages,
dead letters, and about what never ages.

Black Powder

for Kate

Saltpeter, to sailors who swore the cooks
put it in the eggs to keep their cocks in check;
Nitre, to alchemists who dreamed
of turning lead to gold;
Potassium Nitrate, to the druggist who asked
the boy what he would do with that.

The ancient Chinese recipe:
Mix with sulfur, charcoal
seven parts to one to two.
Grind it fine as talc.

What he would do is strike a match, then watch
the blaze of self-discovery—
the boyhood burn to master
the forbidden and impossible—
choking the basement with smoke
from what could sink a ship at Scapa Flow.

Aristophanes at Cancún

Running round my kylix rim
the satyr shouts, "So where's the quim?"
Pornai work the New York docks
for disembarking sailors' cocks.
Courtesans, with more to sell,
cajole their Wall Street clientele.
From Burning Man to Lauderdale,
the Bacchanal's alive and well.

But what of this religious fuss
at anything that smacks of lust?
The priests who send all sex to Hell
with holy water and tinkling bell
did not lead the well-hung bull
To ithyphallic Festival.
One eye out for Hera, Zeus
considers who he'll next seduce.

Promethean

It was anger—the audacious theft—
that chained him to the cliff for vulture's fare.
But fire itself, Zeus knew, could be the more
poetic punishment: subvert the gift
to a burning underground—Kentucky coal seams,
the slow combustion of mass burials
stoking the decay with human fuel
in plague pits, under soccer stadiums;
make it the incinerating blooms
of Bikini, Fukushima, and Chernobyl,
the Willie Pete and Little Boy that fell
on Dresden, Hiroshima, Vietnam.
Make him the airman crouched above his sight,
aiming to illuminate the night.

In a Taverna

In Greek mythology Leda was visited by Zeus in the form of a swan. Their union produced two eggs, from which came Helen of Troy and Clytemnestra. Europa was visited by Zeus in the form of a white bull. Three children resulted, all of whom became kings. Apollo sought to seduce Cassandra by giving her the power of prophesy. When she refused him he spat into her mouth, with the curse that no one would believe her prophecies. She foresaw the fall of Troy. Agamemnon married Clytemnestra after murdering her husband. When he returned from Troy with Cassandra as a war prize, he was murdered by Clytemnestra.

Leda:	It wasn't a matter of choice, really.
Europa:	Do they ever ask?
Cassandra:	Try saying No. He spat in my mouth!
Leda:	Of course, the attention is flattering.
Europa:	"The man's desire is for the woman, the woman's desire is for the desire of the man."
Leda:	That goes double for a god.
Cassandra:	[*Shudders*] To be the sex slave of a god . . .
Leda:	is something to be remembered for.
Europa:	I had to tell my husband something. He knew they weren't his.
Leda:	And how else to explain why I laid eggs?
Cassandra:	How awful. What was it like?
Leda:	Laying eggs? Painful.
Cassandra:	No, fornication with a god.
Leda:	More painful.
Europa:	At least you had a swan. Try a bull.
Cassandra:	What was *that* like?

Leda:	Don't say you didn't enjoy it.
Europa:	Well, it's not the kind of thing you forget.
Cassandra:	And the children never turn out.
Leda:	I beg your pardon. My Helen . . .
Cassandra:	The face that sank a thousand ships.
	[*To Europa*] Three times your loins fired . . .
Europa:	. . . and three times Kings came out.
Leda:	And my Clytemnestra?
Cassandra:	Whore to whoring Agamemnon.
Leda:	And you were not?
Cassandra:	I was his *war* prize. You think he asked?
Europa:	Agamemnon: Dead and so deserving.
	It's a pity gods can't die.
Leda:	Mortal, immortal, they're all the same.
	Waiter! More retsina.

Chicago, Tell Me Who You Are

I'm a city with a past, a memory
of fire. No fear is like the fear
of a wooden city on a windy day.
Even the people were on fire. "Throw me in the river,"
she told her husband. "I'd rather drown than burn."

I'm Lincoln when he stands for President.
I'm the *City of Big Shoulders* and the World's Fair.
I'm Millennium Park and the long lakeshore,
the Magnificent Mile and tallest towers.
The Cubs and White Sox, Bulls and Bears.

I'm Baby Face, Capone, and Dillinger;
Sandburg, Gwen Brooks, Hemingway;
Disney, Orson Welles, and Tina Fey;
Oprah, Smashing Pumpkins, Nat King Cole;
Jack Benny, Belushi, and Steve Colbert.

I'm "Sunday in the Park" and George Seurat;
the Symphony of Reiner and Solti;
Sinatra and *Chicago, Chicago,*
they have the time, the time of their life.
I saw a man, he danced with his wife!

The world's planes converge on me.
Flaps extending, each one flowers as it lands.
Astronauts in space see
a city risen from an inland sea.
My hands are filled with phosphorescent dreams.

The Power & Light Company

for Mary K. Mcintire

Under the Used and Useful Principle
a public utility may charge customers
only for assets that are used and useful
in providing service to those who pay for it:
power plants, transmission lines, the sum total
of what it takes to deliver power and light.

Most of those with needs for power and light
in their lives work from a different principle.
Power—prerogative with impunity—is total
by nature, not a thing to sell to customers.
Those who gain it keep it. Having it
befits them, whether used or useful.

Light, on the other hand, is useful
when it gives illumination; think how light
reflecting off the moon reveals it, renders it.
Whether gaining and keeping is the principle
or giving is, matters to customers.
The one's cost, the other's benefit is total.

Can those receiving service unbundle the total,
choosing the light, which is nothing if not useful,
but not the power which is not for sale to customers
in any case? Does having the light
without the power offend some principle
of commerce? If so, are we compelled to honor it?

Power, we know, excoriates what it
can't control; antipathy is total
and portends the death of principle.
If we take only the light, can it be useful
without the power? If not, of what use is the light?
That is the quandary for customers.

And face it, our lot is to be customers:
Something received, things taken in return for it.
Light without power or power without light.
How do we keep the dark from turning total
when we ourselves would be the used and useful?
When giving our lives a purpose is the principle?

Caveat emptor, customers. The game is total,
your lives for it: You will be used if you are useful.
But as to power and light, let light be principal.

Emerging Market Unicorn

A startup worth $1 billion is rare, a so-called unicorn.

He hears the whistle of the Wall Street man
and wonders what this latest call might mean.

After centuries on the British Crest,
Christian longings that the mythical
appear and validate a miracle,
must royalty and abbots now make space
for investors and the marketplace?

If equity means merely owned, not just,
and interest only means the bankers' kind,
he sees a trend: how this will be the end
of faith, analysts will measure cost
but not the cost of noble hopes once lost.

He snorts. It will be easy to resist
once more his ancient hunger to exist.

Song of the Newlyweds

for Jenny and Tony

We slept until the clocks ran down,
the wedding flowers dried to dust,
the gas man disconnected us.
Days without sound
the spiders darned and starved.

The world returned to work but we did not.
Steeply slanted into sleep,
dream after dream as things should be,
we followed the overtures of our vows
on tides of understanding to where two
together is sufficient and entire,
and marriage a radiant equipoise.

Our quest—for nothing less
than Eden and its innocence—embraced
exalted gardens all across the earth.
But innocence, we learned at last,
is not a state of grace we lose at birth,
then work a lifetime to recover.
It's what a lifelong hunger self-creates.
At the ending of love's labors, ours and yours,
it is the blessing that awaits.

II

The Boxer of Quirinal

The Boxer of Quirinal

For two gross of statues,
  For a few thousand battered books.
—Ezra Pound

When Goths cut the aqueduct
the Romans buried you with care—
a bronze presence to protect.
Lost a millennium and more,

you were found, foundry-perfect:
hide-wrapped hands, ruined head—
battered nose, ears, neck
still fresh with copper flecks of blood.

You look up, spent utterly
by what laurels cost the victor,
see with an explosive vacancy
Europe girding for the Great War.

Dante at Shiloh

I.

I found myself in the aftermath.
Cannonades had set the woods ablaze,
felled whole trees, swept the earth

with canister and grape. From bodies
and body parts heaped up by musketry
(*Aim low and be deliberate, boys.*)

a strangeling crawled—Blue or Gray
I couldn't tell—from the Minié balls' last meal.
Straining to break their cannon free,

dead horses, still in harness, hauled.
Voices out of the burning undergrowth
wept for water as the field fell still.

At the iron dice of war, both sides lost.
Wild pigs won, squabbling over their feast.

II.

It started to rain and with it came a troupe
of orators—men of God,
carpetbaggers of every stripe.

Gingerly, to avoid the mud,
they stepped from one corpse to the next,
crossing the swamp, slipping on blood.

One started to speak, "Brethren in Christ . . ."
but stopped, perplexed, to see another man
wearing his face. This progressed,

speaker after speaker, until soon
each searched in panic through the group,
and when he found his stolen face, that one

he mounted and buggered, like boar on boar—
in self-love or -loathing, I wasn't sure.

The Hove

Such as there was in the littleness of that dawn
could not be this. Not, certainly, the hove
of an invasion fleet from Angleterre,
flotilla wrought by shipwright, chandler, armorer
as if Ice Age breeding stocks were on the move.

The Planners had their weather oracles,
haruspices their entrails. All divined
the red planet aligned, full-moon
visibility, high tides to clear
the beachhead obstacles—but iffy weather.

Gulls glean the wakes. Something of a factory—
diesel and air and the Jersey spirit spark—
of the hydrocarbon *Gloriana* makes
ungainly way in the valleys of the swells.
The shore emerges quaquaversally.

A Very pistol throats the air. Battlewagons
wheel for the presentation of the agon.
Shades of sherry flood the clouds with light.
Mike boats enter surf's unscrolling rolls.
Empty jaws agape, the gods take note.

The odors of the offering, so rich
they start saliva flowing, must be painful
for the gods: Not preamble for the meal,
the meal itself. Famished
they try to gorge the oily cooking smoke.

Amphibious landings to prevail require
the triumph of the small; circle in circle
perfected on parade grounds of the soul.
Committing an empire to the fire
calls for Just-in-Time ferocity.

They eat the savage honey. The boys pound sand.
Green eyes gammoning they all pound sand
until for the battle there was nothing left that day
but what the carrion patrols collect
for Paternosterers to sacristy.

They're strong, these Irish Penny Whistle songs.
Just the one wild tone working alone
the registers, trying the proper sound
for sorrow. Ours for theirs,
theirs for theirs, ours for ours.

So many shouldering forward, enjambed
now cross the Styx with the ease of smoke
passing through a window screen . . . depart
the shapes of things continuing for shapes
supercooled to the stillness of mortmain.

The business of the flag is never done.
It fills in the wind and fails, but never the same
akimbo twice. Each snap a fresh report
from acres of tended lawn
rankled by crosses perfectly plumb.

Ship Captain Crew

USS Warrington *(1945–1972)*

I.

What is a ship on the ways
but twenty-seven hundred tons
of waiting steel, a maze

of empty bunks and unworked guns?
No captain? No resolve.
No crew? No dash, no muscle—no means.

But plankowners arrive,
fire the boilers, take in line—
shake the ship alive.

More than iron, more than human,
ship captain crew bond
and out of three emerges one:

Bessemer-built and -boned,
a man o' war that hauls and sails
wherever missions command.

II.

A month out of Newport, monsoon swells,
the storms of Tonkin Gulf.
Rain, fog, the midwatch bells,

and—somewhere—Pratas Reef:
graveyard for ships whose lookouts fail
to see its breaking surf.

Off North Vietnam, gun line patrol,
the still waters erupt—
two mines explode beneath her hull.

Engines wrecked, pipes
ruptured, flooding, listing port—
the crew reclaims the ship,

pumps and patches, keeps her afloat
and headed East Sou'-East
for the tow to Subic and her fate.

III.

Condemned, struck from the List,
sold for parts and scrap. To Taiwan
breaking yards released.

Work of the cutting torches done,
fed to furnaces,
the atoms in her metals find

an afterlife as traces—
a small part on a ship perhaps,
a hawse pipe or a windlass.

And what of a crew without its ship?
Sailors grow old, go on
as atoms—all things go on, except

for this: The mythic bond—
a beast half steel half soul—gone
never to return.

The South China Sea

Introduction

The South China Sea has turned into an international flash-point as Chinese leaders insist with increasing truculence that its islands, rocks, and reefs have been China's historical territory since ancient times.
> —Professor Mohan Malik
> June 2013

The world will not allow Beijing to treat the South China Sea as its maritime empire.
> —US Secretary of State Pompeo
> July 13, 2020

Possession is nine-tenths of the Law.
> —Adage

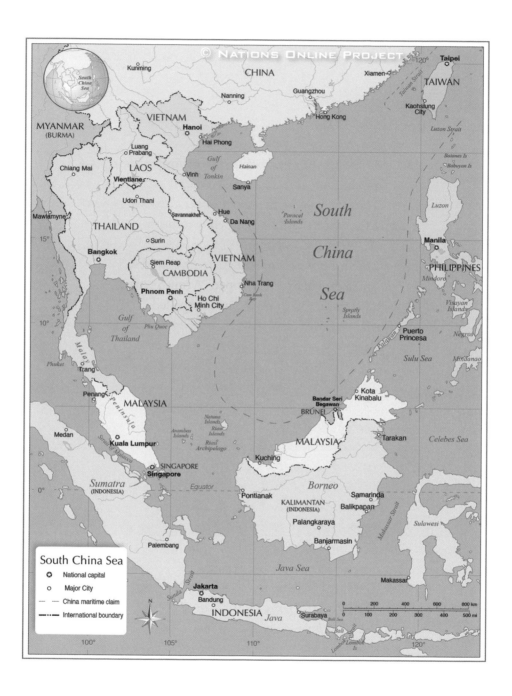

The Colonist

I wake to the sound of surf. Nothing to see
in all directions but the level sea.
I'm sitting on a tall aluminum chair,
lifeguard-like. I climb down to a tumble
of Jerry cans and boxes on the sand:
Drinking water, matches, fish hooks, line,
and a case of Spam stamped "Army Surplus."
And a letter with my name misspelled.

Comrade, by now you must be wondering
where you are, how you got here, and why.
You've been selected for a vital task.
For far too long China's sovereignty
over the South China Sea—all
its islands, atolls, rocks, reefs, and shoals—
has been disputed by upstart neighbor states.
Vietnam, the Philippines, even
lowly Brunei have asserted claims
on these barren, uninhabited places
(and any oil reserves that lie beneath).

The People's Republic has been patient. But now
the UN Conference on the Law of the Sea,
the machinations of the Seventh Fleet
(those running dogs), and domestic considerations
make it urgent to perfect our case.

Possession being nine-tenths of the law,
we have determined to found a colony!
A colony requires a colonist,
and that's where you come in: a colonist
with evidence of permanent residence.

We needed a turnkey citizen, someone
without attachments who would not be missed.
We found you, passed out in the Transit Lounge
at Shanghai Airport, your face in a bowl of soba.
Your papers said "No living relatives."
On the spot we decided you would do.
You'll never be a true Chinese, of course,
but we've made you an honorary citizen,
the South China Sea's first colonist!
Your mission starts today. Raise our flag,
take selfies cheering and saluting it.
Plant the seeds from our supplies—the beans,
the corn, the cabbages—a Victory Garden!
Keep a daily journal of your exploits,
make it patriotic and persuasive.
Your place in history is guaranteed.
You'll be valorized! Eternalized!
Tempis fugit, Comrade. Now get to work.

Colonel Gee Haw
Acting Territorial Administrator
for the Chinese Communist Party
South China Sea

His Journal

Day 1

The South China Sea: Tectonic tears
of the earth, sprinkled with casts from the Sower's hand.
Out of the throat of a caldera's collapse
my atoll makes a mouth, an anguished O.
It takes an hour to walk the surf's surround.

Grounded wrecks, surf-eaten from within,
present their bowsprits. The reef as taxidermist.
Says the Coral: *We build on the skeletons*
of elders, rise from the deep, wait for ships
to lose their bearings in the sound of surf
improperly near. We hear the graveyard watch,
their shouts, then the slam, the fragility
of steel on our unreckoned fact. Some drown,
some swim. We razor survivors' naked soles.

Day 2

Bowl in hand I scavenge beach debris,
pick for orts through mounds of ruckled gunk.
Fish heads, seaweed, bird bones, vacated shells . . .
it doesn't help to be omnivorous here.

I stalk blowholes, try tidal pools
busy as a blender on Saturday night.

The black-and-neon Sergeant Majors—too quick
for me—nibble coral, shit sand.

Day 3

Between the dead and the quick I have more luck.
The black anger of a hooked cod.
A turtle in a consternation of bubbles.
The toasted lozenge of a sea cucumber.
I make slumgullion: a can of Spam,
add the corn, the beans, the cabbage sprouts
they left for me to grow a garden with.

Day 11

Life here moves according to the moon,
each night waxing more, reaching for
the rendezvous. Full and perigee,
it nods: *Yes, tonight. Tonight's the night.*
Crabs emerge tantivy from the surf,
a shellback army summoned for the spawn.

I step back from the swarm, climb my perch.
In the melee below I can't distinguish
the reproductive grip of claws on claws
from the mortal grip of claws on rival claws.
At dawn the gravid and crippled crawl for the tide.
Club in hand I collect my evening meal.

Day 20

Days clone days. The sun's formative fury
burns me shades of sherry, lobster bisque.
My starveling stomach's taut as a drum. I eke.
Lacking options the body feeds on itself,
fat first, as it should, then muscle
down to a core, surviving just because.
Existence is not enoughness. "There's more to life
than this," I say to no one in particular.

Day 21

Birds have left without a song.
Morning light looks yellow and wrong.
"Bring what you must," I tell Monsoon,
"Anything—except Typhoon."

"I am come," Typhoon replies.
"Thunderstorms devour your skies,
Lightning plays its brisk staccato
Over thunder's obbligato.

"Atoll's unprotected face
Cannot hide from my embrace."
Combers grow gargantuan,
bury the reef again, again.

Palm trees buckle in gale-force winds,
Earth revisits its origins.
Islands tremble in the shock,
Continental plates undock.

Chaos with a long release
Unmakes planet piece by piece.

And I only am escaped alone to tell thee.

The surf recedes to its monotony.
The reef gets on with its 10,000 years.
Tower gone, food and water gone,
I lay me down. Time to study how
to will the beating of a heart to cease.
Crabs gather, gulls and boobies gather:
a shrinking circle of the famished drawn
to the savage honey of a stricken man.

Delirious, I hallucinate,
see a mirage—a life raft in the shallows.
A man crawls out, totters to where I lie.
"Are you alive?" he asks.
                              "Are you?"
"I was standing lookout when a wave
big as a house carried me overboard
with everything—the life raft, too. I'm Skobrak,
Sonarman from the destroyer *Warrington*."

He gives me water, rations from his raft.
Orphans of the storm, we beach the boat,
right the tower, unload survival gear:
K-rations, fishing tackle, signal mirror.
A Very pistol and a dozen flares;
one whistle and one American flag.

That afternoon we spot a plane. It sees us,
flies in for a look. Frantically
we fire a flare, activate the beacon.
It makes a low pass, wiggles its wings in reply.
We raise the American flag, upside down.
It makes repeated passes, then flies off.
That night we celebrate with chocolate bars.

Running Dogs & Capitalist Roaders

Next day more planes come boring in. All day
we wait. At dusk two ships appear,
coming fast from opposite directions.
They hove-to off our atoll a mile apart.
We tune our shortwave radio to hear
how the rescue will proceed.

"AMERICAN SHIP, IDENTIFY YOURSELF."

"THIS IS USS *WARRINGTON*.
IDENTIFY YOURSELF."

"DESTROYER *QIN SHI HUANG*. YOU ARE HERE
WITHOUT PERMISSION OR AUTHORITY
IN TERRITORIES OF THE PRC.
CLEAR THIS AREA IMMEDIATELY!"

"WE DO NOT RECOGNIZE YOUR CLAIM.
THESE ARE INTERNATIONAL WATERS, OPEN
BY TREATY UNDER FREEDOM OF THE SEA."

"REPEAT, CLEAR THIS AREA IMMEDIATELY."

"WE ARE HERE ON A RESCUE OPERATION.
WE HEAR THE RADIO BEACON LOUD AND CLEAR.
DO NOT INTERFERE WITH THE SEVENTH FLEET."

"CAPITALIST DOGS, YOU LIE! YOUR FLAG NOW FLIES
ABOVE OUR COLONY. WE HAVE THE PHOTOS.
YOU ARE INVADERS. YOU HAVE SEIZED AN OUTPOST
ON OUR LANDS AND RAISED THE STARS AND STRIPES."

The Gods of War

With twilight closing in, more ships arrive:
gray hulls of the Seventh Fleet,
gray hulls of the Chinese Coastal Fleet.
Opposing columns make ready to engage.
Ships swing, unmasking batteries,
bringing torpedo tubes to bear.
From circling planes, flares and float lights drop.
Thin white cones of searchlights probe where ships
show battle lights: green-over-white-over-green.
The ocean glistens with a delicate sheen.

Each side claims the other fired first.
In the soft dark, sudden muzzle flashes,
tracers arching orange across the sky,
star shells falling terrible and red
like the gates of hell opening, closing.

One turns—*All ahead flank! Hard right rudder!*—
and combs the wakes of a spread of torpedoes.
One registers the sullen glow of hits.
A massive explosion in her magazines
blossoms skyward, engulfs her broken bow.
Then firing ceases, sudden as it began.

Daybreak. Flotsam where a ship went down,
frothing waters dotted with bobbing heads.

Ships and sharks converge, contend
if these be souls to save or helpless bait.

Ptolemy would have recognized the scene:
Two men on an atoll sit for days,
the unmoving center of a universe
of ships, poised as the gods of war look on.

Enter diplomacy. At noon sharp
two boats lower and depart their ships.
Armed sailors land them on the beach.
One takes Skobrak back to *Warrington*.
The other takes me to the Chinese fleet.

The Law of the Sea

"This UN Conference on the Law of the Sea
has been convened to adjudicate the claim
of China to the South China Sea
with all attendant islands, atolls, reefs.
The disputants have made their closing statements:
Vietnam, Malaysia, the Philippines,
Indonesia, Taiwan, and Brunei.
The United States has moved to reject China's claim
and condemn its recent, lawless belligerence.
Before the vote we'll hear from the PRC."

"I am Colonel Gee. My government
has charged me to present our final statement.
Our case, you know already, is compelling.
But one thing makes it incontestable.
My country, alone among the disputants,
has established a permanent colony
on an island in the China Sea.
Since possession is nine-tenths of the law,
our sovereignty is indisputable.
Our flag now flies above a settlement
where gardens of beans, corn, cabbages
are flourishing. But please don't take my word.
Here to offer witness is our founding
colonist, the living proof. Comrade?"

"I should clarify my friendship with Colonel Gee.
I'm not a citizen of the PRC.
Changing planes in Shanghai, I ate a bowl
of soba and blacked out at Security.
I was drugged. Kidnapped. Threatened. Shanghaied.
I woke on an atoll at the end of the world.
I had shipwrecked ghosts for company.
I fought the gulls and boobies for their fish.
There are no gardens. I ate the beans, the corn,
the cabbage sprouts–oh, and a case of Spam.
There was a camp—a typhoon took that, too."

"This is regrettable, and none of it true.
A US warship tried to seize our colony,
a flagrant challenge to our sovereignty.
They even raised their flag—we have the photos!"

"It's true we raised the flag—but upside down,
the international signal of distress!
China wants another inch of map
but nothing there belongs to humankind.
That place already has been 'colonized,'
the CCP will merely ape the crabs.
Despite panjandrum edicts and demands,
undocumented winds blow where they will;
endless lines of surf without a censor
have their say. Out there Nature makes
the only laws. The only sovereignty:
the plus-nothing of the open surge."

The Second Colonist

Those running dogs in Beijing put me here,
their scapegoat for the UN Conference vote.
But I will not despair. I am Gee,
the star of State Surveillance. soon to be
Master of the South China Sea!

To plan my return a long walk on the beach
will do me good, will concentrate my mind.
The moon is full and, Oh, so large tonight,
it must be near. But what's that in the surf?
Crabs? Millions of them, an army of crabs
swarming up the beach! They're on my feet!

III

The Immortality Sweepstakes

Stump Work

They sell a stew of chemicals to rot
the stump, like quicklime on dishonored dead.
You burn what's left. This will not do.

Its bole held crown and root
against a century of wind and drought;
carried life—we never could,
not Orpheus, not Eurydice—
to this world from the one beneath.

Get the axe, give it the death
that is a noble's due.

Obsequy

Who built Longfellow's House?
History of the long bow.
The last eruption of Vesuvius.

If his going took from us
nothing not on Wikipedia,
what is our loss?

What is lost
when a hawk, curious
or hungry, lifts from its tree?

The First Emperor

The tomb of Qin Shi Huang (259–210 BC)
was discovered in March 1974.

Nothing if not careful, Qin Shi Huang,
Master of All Under Heaven, spent his reign
ensuring he would live forever.

Thirty-eight years work never ceased
on his necropolis: city-sized model of his Empire—
plains and mountains, the Great Wall and beyond.

The Yellow and Yangtze flowed in mercury
(elixir, water of immortality)
down to seas of mercury.

Gems in the ceiling fired the firmament,
candles of whale oil, big as men, lighted
the sarcophagal center of the universe.

Defended by terracotta soldiery
(generals in chariots with war drums,
pikemen, bowmen, infantry);

protected by spells of sorcerers,
by booby traps (for tomb robbers
crossbows on hair triggers).

Necropolis complete, artisans and work gangs
buried alive to keep its secrets safe,
a mountain raised to hide the site.

Quicksilver pills he took with wine would—
his alchemists guaranteed—prolong his life
at least a hundred centuries . . .

but speech faltered, fingers fumbled.
Qin Shi Huang, First Emperor,
dead of erethism at 49.

Necropolis lost 2000 years,
discovered by farmers digging wells,
the tomb remains unopened to this day.

For all we know he may be reigning in there still:
a day sail down the Yangtze to the sea,
tonight magicians, strongmen, acrobats.

Concubines, interred to please his every whim,
toast another perfect day, pretending
not to hear distant shovels, the tinkle of picks.

Hospice, Morristown NJ

for my brother

Tubing reaches down to feed
each still body on its bed.
Monitors report, report
the cowed persistence of a heart.
Anger . . . loving . . . grieving—gone
to only this: holding on.

Wheeled out to the garden grounds,
they sit among the blooms and fronds
transfixed. What they alone can see:
a mile away, a mile high,
a glacier advances, filling its jaws
with rubble of all that ever was.

Water's Way

It takes 500 years for the ocean's water
to complete one trip around the earth.
—National Geographic Society

The prodigal returned, a bride running late,
it races from the street,
climbs the plumbing in the walls
to the bathroom tap, then halts.

Water is weather. Pulled from swells
out where cyclones make the only news,
its vapor ladders latitudes to the pole,
refreshes bergy bits, brash ice, floes—

or crosses longitudes to fall
as *shoures soote* upon us all,
then drain away to aquifer.
Weather is God's will writ small.

Water is extended metaphor:
Its antecedent, alchemic character
commonly denominates
all things, in compound or by temperature.

4 a.m. Fill the glass.
Let the molecule from Christ
stand again in human state
even as it quenches thirst.

Noel

And there were shepherds abiding in the field,
keeping watch over their flock by night.
(Luke 2:8)

To them Orion was not a huntsman
but a shepherd of the lambent.

Safe from Leo, Lupus, Taurus
his charges followed him to dawn,

counted and content
to know they would persist

when daylight
rendered them no longer visible.

Not souls—not yet—they were signifiers
ready to be metaphors.

Noble Rot

A fungus, fittingly called "noble rot,"
takes hold in vineyards at the end of harvest time.
—Robert Parker

At season's end
a few are left on the vine
to mold and frost.

Gathered by hand
for harvest wine,
yielding perhaps a single glass

at meal's end—
as I would be: wizened
and full of nothing but sweetness.

The Immortality Sweepstakes

Home burial is what I have in mind.
Not a cadaver in the flower bed
but a buried jar with a swipe of DNA
and a note: *Available for cloning.*
                     Elderly gent writes poetry
                     but never learned to dance.
And a headstone with its epitaph:
                     You won't shut me up this easily.
And maybe, on acid-free paper, a copy of this.

Poetry's pursuit is permanence.
Flotsam on oceans of the digital,
our poems scheme to stay discoverable.
If not, *Carve the runes, then be content with silence.*

What exactly do we mean, *survive*?
Realia? Washington's false teeth.
Remains? The lead coffin of John Paul Jones,
recovered from a forgotten cemetery,
reinterred as the Father of Our Navy.
What do we mean by *immortality*?

In 1974 a hominin,
Australopithecus africanus,
was discovered in Ethiopia.
The skeleton, 40 percent complete,
three million years old, caused a sensation.
A world tour followed. Lucky Lucy.

Notes

The Governing Reality
The final couplet is from Yeats, "The Circus Animals' Desertion."

Promethean
The first hydrogen bomb was tested on Bikini Atoll. Major nuclear power accidents occurred at Fukushima and Chernobyl. Willie Pete is military parlance for white phosphorus, used in incendiary bombs. Little Boy was the code name for the atomic bomb dropped on Hiroshima.

The Hove
The Normandy Landings, D-Day 1944, the beginning of the end of WWII in Europe.

The South China Sea
"The Gods of War" draws on eye-witness accounts of the Naval Battle of Guadalcanal, a series of night engagements between fleets of the Imperial Japanese Navy and the US Navy in November 1942.

Ship Captain Crew
USS *Warrington* (DD843) was built and launched at the end of WWII. An East coast destroyer, she made her first deployment to the Vietnam War in 1966. Five years later, with a different crew, she made a second deployment to the gun line in Tonkin Gulf, where she was severely damaged by underwater mines. Her crew saved the ship and kept her afloat during the tow back to Subic, where she was decommissioned and sold for scrap. This poem was written for a fiftieth reunion of my shipmates from that first cruise: Ron Wills, Jim Morgan, Bill Moore, Cliff Hayes, Pete Lothrop.

Stump Work

In medieval times when execution of commoners was by hanging, nobles had the right to choose beheading, by axe or sword.

The Immortality Sweepstakes

CARVE THE RUNES, THEN BE CONTENT WITH SILENCE:
The epitaph on the headstone of the Scottish poet George Mackay Brown.
The hominin was named *Lucy* by her discoverers, who celebrated all night to "Lucy in the Sky with Diamonds" blasting at full volume.

Biographical Note

John Barr was born in Omaha, Nebraska, and grew up in a rural township outside of Chicago. A graduate of Harvard College and Harvard Business School, he served as a Navy officer on destroyers for five years, which included three tours to Vietnam. In a thirty-year career as an investment banker, he was a managing director of Morgan Stanley and founded three startups. He has taught in the Graduate Writing Program at Sarah Lawrence College and served on the boards of Yaddo, Bennington College, and the Poetry Society of America, the latter two as board chair. In 2004 he was appointed inaugural president of the Poetry Foundation, publisher of *Poetry* magazine, and served in that capacity for its first decade.

Over the past thirty years Barr's poems have been published in three books by Red Hen Press (*Dante in China, The Hundred Fathom Curve: New & Collected Poems*, and *The Adventures of Ibn Opcit*, a two-volume mock epic); two books by Story Line Press (*The Hundred Fathom Curve* and *Grace*); and four hand-printed editions by Warwick Press (*The War Zone, Natural Wonders, The Dial Painters*, and *Centennial Suite*). *The Boxer of Quirinal* is his tenth book.